F MY LIFE
WORLD TOUR

F MY LIFE
WORLD TOUR

Life's Crappiest Moments
from Around the Globe

MAXIME VALETTE,
GUILLAUME PASSAGLIA,
AND DIDIER GUEDJ

A Perigee Book

A PERIGEE BOOK
Published by the Penguin Group
Penguin Group (USA) Inc.
375 Hudson Street, New York, New York 10014, USA
Penguin Group (Canada), 90 Eglinton Avenue East, Suite 700, Toronto, Ontario M4P 2Y3, Canada
(a division of Pearson Penguin Canada Inc.) • Penguin Books Ltd., 80 Strand, London WC2R 0RL,
England • Penguin Group Ireland, 25 St. Stephen's Green, Dublin 2, Ireland (a division of Penguin
Books Ltd.) • Penguin Group (Australia), 250 Camberwell Road, Camberwell, Victoria 3124, Australia
(a division of Pearson Australia Group Pty. Ltd.) • Penguin Books India Pvt. Ltd., 11 Community
Centre, Panchsheel Park, New Delhi—110 017, India • Penguin Group (NZ), 67 Apollo Drive,
Rosedale, Auckland 0632, New Zealand (a division of Pearson New Zealand Ltd.) • Penguin Books
(South Africa) (Pty.) Ltd., 24 Sturdee Avenue, Rosebank, Johannesburg 2196, South Africa

Penguin Books Ltd., Registered Offices: 80 Strand, London WC2R 0RL, England

While the authors have made every effort to provide accurate telephone numbers and Internet addresses
at the time of publication, neither the publisher nor the authors assume any responsibility for errors or
for changes that occur after publication. Further, the publisher does not have any control over and
does not assume any responsibility for author or third-party websites or their content.

Copyright © 2012 by Maxime Valette, Guillaume Passaglia, and Didier Guedj
Illustrations by Marie Levesque

First edition: June 2012

Library of Congress Cataloging-in-Publication Data

Valette, Maxime, 1988–
F my life world tour : life's crappiest moments from around the world / Maxime Valette,
Guillaume Passaglia, Didier Guedj.
p.   cm.
"A Perigee book."
ISBN 978-0-399-16010-3 (pbk.)
1. Conduct of life—Humor.   2. Embarrassment—Humor.   I. Passaglia, Guillaume, 1982–.   II. Guedj,
Didier.   III. Title.
PN6231.C6142V358   2012
818'.60208—dc23   2012010469

PRINTED IN THE UNITED STATES OF AMERICA

10 9 8 7 6 5 4 3 2 1

Most Perigee books are available at special quantity discounts for bulk
purchases for sales promotions, premiums, fund-raising, or educational use. Special books,
or book excerpts, can also be created to fit specific needs. For details, write: Special Markets,
Penguin Group (USA) Inc., 375 Hudson Street, New York, New York 10014.

CONTENTS

F MY LIFE
WORLD TOUR

INTRODUCTION

The blame for all this belongs to Maxime. Back in 2008, he started sharing stories of embarrassing and awkward moments with a few friends online. Since other people's misfortunes bring pleasure to whoever is watching from the sidelines, more and more intrigued people started turning up to read them, often adding their own humbling moments to the mix. And, thus, FML was born. Maxime was quickly joined by Guillaume, and then Didier. To our surprise, what started out as a European phenomenon quickly grew into a global sensation, with thousands of FMLs sent in every day. Today, we get more than 2.2 million visits a day, from Web and app users around the world.

And as the book you're reading demonstrates, we get submissions from around the world, too. It's as if crappy luck, everyday nuisances, and life's ironic little twists of fate are the universal language.

If you're looking for truly hard-luck stories, take note: We traffic in cringe-worthy little moments, not major atrocities; we publish only those items that fit into the categories of self-deprecation, embarrassment, and whatever makes us chuckle. Now it's your turn to relish them.

ASIA

MALAYSIA

Today, I learned that if you accidentally sit on a hamster, instead of dying, it bites your testicles. FML

Today, I found out that my girlfriend has more armpit hair than I do. FML

Today, someone switched my hair spray with bug spray. I discovered this too late. FML

Today, I popped a huge zit on my nose, and the pus squirted into my eye. FML

Today, I wrapped a towel around my waist so I could take a dump while using my laptop. I sat on the toilet seat and let a big load go. Turns out I forgot to unwrap the towel. FML

INDONESIA

Today, when I proposed to my girlfriend of eight years, she said no because she thought we were moving too fast. FML

Today, it's my birthday. I'm a pastry chef by profession. Not only did my family buy a cake from my bakery, I had to make it myself and inscribe it with "Happy Birthday Dad." The worst part is, they asked for money from me to pay for it. FML

PHILIPPINES

Today, my boyfriend broke up with me through Skype, with the message "my penis wants more, but my heart and mind don't want to hurt you." WTF? FML

Today, my family and I went to the mall. We all split up in a department store to shop for our own clothes. While shopping, I caught my dad feeling up a mannequin in the back corner of the store. FML

Today, I went to the mall and couldn't find a parking spot. After circling around for 20 minutes, I finally saw a shaded spot under a tree. It turns out I parked under a coconut tree. I could tell from the coconut embedded into my hood. FML

Today, I was sitting in my garden and having a cup of tea while watching some dragonflies. I thought the dragon-flies were really pretty, so I ran toward them and tried to catch their tails like I used to when I was a kid. They were exotic wasps. FML

Today, my friends and I went out drinking, and luckily enough, the guy I've had a crush on for the past four years was there. I decided to get drunk so that I could make a move and blame it on the alcohol. I went in to whisper my confession in his ear . . . only to puke on him. FML

THAILAND

Today, my shrink diagnosed me as severely depressive, due to a lot of stress and yelling at home. After the session, my parents argued about whose fault it was and then went on to yell at me for being depressive and wasting their money. FML

Today, I was playing with my yo-yo. I began showing off to my friends. When the girl I have a crush on walked by, I thought it'd be really cool to do the move "dog bite." I ended up hitting myself in the balls. Hard. FML

CAMBODIA

Today, while celebrating my birthday with my friends and family, I met a girl at the bar who seemed interested. She got up and left after my mother whispered in her ear, "If you go home with my son, make sure he wears a condom." FML

INDIA

Today, I was peacefully journaling, reflecting, and enjoying the beautiful landscape. And then a monkey threw its poo at me. FML

Today, I went to a meditation center for some much-needed relaxation. I drove for an hour and then walked around in the scorching sun for two more hours trying to locate the damn place. I returned home angrier than ever. FML

CHINA

Today, I was pouring boiling tea into a thermos to take to work, when I saw my neighbor walking her dog. She waved at me, and I waved back. I forgot that I had a thermos in my hand, and I waved it all over myself, causing burns over my face and most of my body. FML

Today, after nine months in our relationship, my boyfriend and I lost our virginity to each other. We had incredible, mind-blowing sex. An hour later, he broke up with me because apparently my "orgasm face is ugly." FML

Today, I was at my girlfriend's house for dinner. Her mom served me some seasoned broccoli, which I didn't like. Not wanting to insult her, I slid the broccoli off my plate and gave it to their dog. It turns out broccoli gives the dog explosive diarrhea. FML

Today, I was going to have sex with my boyfriend, who's Hispanic. Wanting to turn him on, I had asked my friend how to say "fuck me" in Spanish. She claimed it was "pollo frito." I then proceeded to have sex, screaming "pollo frito" for an hour. I later realized I was screaming "fried chicken." FML

Today, I tried a fish pedicure, where the fish swim around your feet and eat the dead skin cells. After 15 minutes of being a human buffet, some of the fish died. FML

JAPAN

Today, I discovered that explosive diarrhea can happen at the most inopportune times, such as on the day of my wedding. At the altar while my husband said his vows. FML

Today, my husband left his cell phone at home. I looked through his contacts and found a person named "The Bitch." Being a very curious person, I decided to call "The Bitch" to see who it was. My phone rang. FML

Today, I saw my train pulling into the station. I sprinted up the stairs and luckily made the train. I looked around and no one was in my compartment. I began to notice that the train was heading down some tracks I'd never been to. I got stuck on an empty train for three hours in the train garage. FML

Today, I was in a store, using the only bathroom there. After I was done, I realized I couldn't open the door. Panicking, I banged on the door and screamed for help. The security guard and a whole group of shoppers gathered, only to find that I was pulling the door instead of pushing it. FML

PAKISTAN

Today, I was eating a packet of chips while watching TV. I saw a crumb on the table in front of me, so without thinking I picked it up and ate it. It wasn't a crumb. It was a tick. FML

Today, I took my friends out to an expensive restaurant for my birthday treat. They had arranged for a surprise birthday cake for me, which I cut, very happily, while they chanted birthday wishes. When the bill came, I discovered I was supposed to pay for my great "surprise" cake. FML

ISRAEL

Today, while I was running around the block, I had the urge to spit. Suddenly I noticed this beautiful girl running in front me. Trying to impress her, I smiled and by mistake drooled everything on the pavement. She wasn't impressed. FML

Today, I was eating at an outdoor restaurant with a few friends. After the waitress cleaned up our table, there was a drop of mayo on the table. I wiped it with my finger and licked it. It wasn't mayo; it was bird shit. FML

Today, I got an "Enlarge your penis" email for the millionth time. I was about to dismiss it when I saw the forwarding address. It was from my wife. FML

Today, my crush of more than a year came over for me to take her on our first date. Today was also the day my parents decided to get drunk and do the chicken dance in our front yard. FML

Today, my mom told me that she doesn't want me to help any of my friends get a job at the restaurant where I work. Apparently, she thinks that they would do a better job than me and get me fired. FML

Today, I had my hair cut and straightened to impress this girl at work. She seemed really impressed and acted really nice to me all of a sudden. Turns out it's just because she thinks I'm gay now. FML

KUWAIT

Today, I was acting as Prince Charming for a five-year-old's birthday party. After my scene at the ball, the narrator asked the kids, "Was the prince handsome?" and they all replied with a chorus of "Nooooo!" FML

EUROPE

SPAIN

Today, I went to a restaurant for lunch. The waiter brought some bread and I started eating it as I waited for him to take my order. A few minutes later, he came back and said, "Don't eat too much bread, honey. It'll make you fatter." I never thought of myself as fat. FML

ITALY

Today, I was locked out of my house. After hours of trying to break the door, I found out I'd accidentally left a window open. The door, however, still needs to be replaced. FML

Today, I was having sex with a girl. She was really into it and not holding back on the noise . . . That is, until I received a text message from my little sister next door reading, "If she is making that much noise, she is probably faking it . . . Trust me, I know." FML

Today, I was riding a stationary exercise bike at home. When I tried to get off, my shorts got stuck under the seat. I dangled half upside down until my shorts ripped and I fell on the ground face-first. I broke my front tooth riding a bike that doesn't even move. FML

GREECE

Today, I was getting my portrait done. The artist told me to smile. He looked at me, then said, "Ohh, don't smile." FML

Today, I spent hours consoling my girlfriend for getting dumped by the guy she was cheating on me with. FML

Today, I said to the pool boy who works at my house, "I know what you're doing and you have to stop it." He started shouting that I had no right to tell them what to do and that they were in love. He was referring to his relationship with my eldest son. I wanted to tell him to stop drinking my beers. FML

POLAND

Today, I was walking in the mountains. I started to trip, so I grabbed onto a fence to soften my fall. The fence was electric. FML

Today, my husband of 10 years was playing The Sims. I asked him about the house he built. Apparently, it was his dream house, and he re-created himself as a Sim so he could live in it. Then I asked him where the wife was. There was no wife. It was his happy place. FML

Today, I fell asleep in history class. I was dreaming about my history teacher. When I woke up, everyone was staring at me rather weirdly and the teacher wasn't there. Turns out I was moaning the teacher's name in my sleep. FML

GERMANY

Today, I decided to take a nap before a big job interview at 6 o'clock. I set two alarm clocks to make sure I didn't miss it, but I woke up at 5:59. As I'm scrambling in a panic to get out the door, my mom says calmly, "I took your alarm clocks out of your room because you looked really tired today." FML

Today, I finally got a date with one of the hottest girls in school, a perfect 10. Just before I go to pick her up to go to the movies, I call her to find out where she lives. She answers the phone, only to hear my father yelling in the background, "Stop talking to that whore." FML

Today, I was at the McDonald's drive-thru getting my morning coffee, when some guy slammed into the back of my car. I was holding the cup between my legs, so now I have second-degree burns on my lady parts. FML

Today, I arrived in my dorm at 3 a.m. to find my roommate passed out and a nauseating stench. While I was gone, he got drunk and puked all over the walls, carpet, and both beds. His inebriated attempt to clean up the mess consisted of smearing his vomit everywhere with my shower robe. FML

Today, I was at a party with my girlfriend, and this older guy came in and started talking to me about his rock climbing lessons earlier that week. I told him, "I'm really drunk, so I really couldn't give a shit about what you did." It was my girlfriend's father picking her up to go home. FML

Today, I met my cousin after two years. She got really tall and skinny, like a model. I joked, saying, "You've grown and gotten slim, and I've stayed the same and have gotten fat." I expected some sort of disagreement. Instead, she looked me up and down, frowned, and gave me a long, sympathetic hug. FML

FINLAND

Today, as I was driving home from work, I noticed a car pulling up next to me, trying to pass me. I sped up, so as not to let him get ahead of me. It took me a while before I realized that I was racing against the shadow of my own car. FML

Today, in the early morning, a worker started drilling right in front of my window. He left five minutes after my alarm clock rang. FML

SWEDEN

Today, while searching a dating site, I came across an account of a girl with the same name and info as myself. She also had the same picture. The girl was me. My life is so loveless that I signed up for the same dating site twice without realizing it. FML

Today, the guy I like called me, and my mom picked up. At the same time, I slipped and fell in the shower and was sitting there moaning. The guy asked if he could speak to me, but my mom heard me and answered, "Well, she is masturbating right now, but I'll tell her to call you later!" FML

Today, the company I've been interviewing for a position with called me. Since I wasn't there to answer, they got my voice mail, in which I'm acting like a drunk David Hasselhoff chewing on a cheeseburger. They called me 12 times. FML

Today, my fiancé gave me an early wedding present. I opened the box and inside was the most adorable cat I've ever seen! It got scared, jumped out, clawed my face, and pissed everywhere. My wedding is tomorrow and I look like Frankenstein's bride. FML

Today, I was at a party where I ate a bowl of disgusting snacks because I didn't want to drink on an empty stomach. I spent the next 12 hours trying to prevent the world from collapsing into millions of demonic shards, because apparently that's what a large dose of magic mushrooms does to you. FML

Today, I was diagnosed with a condition that causes me to have violent diarrhea whenever I get nervous. Now I'm constantly nervous about getting nervous about anything. FML

Today, I was waiting in a long checkout line at the super-market. Behind me were two senior citizens. I felt like doing a good deed, so I said, "Cut ahead of me. I have all the time in the world." The old man scolded me because I supposedly insinuated that they had only a short time left to live. FML

NORWAY

Today, I was at the gym with my boyfriend. He is a bit feminine, but it has never really bothered me. Until I realized I was lifting heavier weights than he was. FML

Today, I was vacuuming our house because I wanted to help my parents. I wore a headset while listening to REALLY loud music. The vacuuming job took me one hour, and when I took off my headset, I noticed that I hadn't plugged in the vacuum cleaner. FML

Today, while standing by the kitchen window, I noticed a mouse running across our lawn on top of the snow. I called my two daughters to come see it, but by the time they got to the window, a hawk was shredding the poor thing to pieces. My kids didn't stop crying for two hours. FML

Today, as I was riding the bus, I saw that an old woman needed help getting off at her stop, so I got up and helped her off. When I finally got her down the stairs, the bus closed its doors and drove away. I was in the middle of nowhere and the bus drove away with all my things. FML

Today, I interviewed potential employees for a job position that I was supposed to get promoted to. FML

Today, I realized that the only thing I learned from my first serious relationship was how to fake an orgasm. FML

Today, I went to the dentist for my yearly teeth cleaning. She took ages trying to clean out my teeth with the metal toothpick thing, constantly hitting my gums. After half an hour of pain and spitting blood, she looked up and said, "Oh, I forgot to put my glasses on." FML

Today, I was trying to wiggle my boxer shorts off to get it on with my girlfriend when my knee hooked on the elastic band. I was anxious to get started, so I used force and ended up kneeing my girlfriend in the crotch. FML

Today, my three-year-old kid wanted to do something nice. I told him he could pick up some of his toys. He gave my new iPhone a bath instead. FML

DENMARK

Today, I was at a concert. When I bent down to tie my shoelace, the girl behind me jumped on my shoulders and refused to get down. She said "tall guys" are the best to ride on during concerts. My name is Maria. FML

Today, my boyfriend brought me home to meet his parents. When they saw me, they laughed. FML

Today, I went to the dentist to get a cavity filled. After the dentist had injected the anesthetic into my gums, she realized that none of the electrical equipment was working. She sent me home. The entire right side of my face is completely numb and swollen for no reason. FML

Today, I was watching a movie with my boyfriend and his parents, who I haven't known very long. At some point I fell asleep, because I woke my drooling self up by snoring extremely loud. FML

IRELAND

Today, I jumped into a pile of snow which had built up against a wall. Turns out it wasn't snow but a pile of cement covered by an inch of snow. FML

Today, the passport office informed me that my new passport won't arrive in time for the vacation I had booked. However, they took the money for the passport out of my bank account two months ago, causing my account to be overdrawn. This means that my travel insurance bill didn't get paid. Which means I can't get the cost of the vacation back. FML

Today, I got dressed up and told my boyfriend that he could do anything he wanted. He said nothing and walked outside. I figured he'd come back in shortly, but when I looked out the window a few minutes later, he was building a snowman. FML

Today, I swapped seats with someone on the ferry so that she could sit next to her friend. Minutes later, a child sitting behind me threw up on my head while the girl I had swapped with laughed hysterically. FML

Today, my dad told me about how my mother had a bad dream last night and screamed, "Don't take me, take my children!" FML

Today, I bought an apartment over what I have just discovered is an Irish folk-music store. FML

NETHERLANDS

Today, I got through to the phone interview stage for a great job. When the phone rang, I answered and suddenly, spontaneously, burped really loudly. The interviewer hung up. FML

Today, I found out my boyfriend's mother has invented a new kind of cake and named it after me: not because it's delicious, but because of the amount of fat in it. FML

Today, when I unhooked my girlfriend's bra, it snapped back and hit me in the eye. FML

BELGIUM

Today, my boyfriend wanted to tell me how much he loves me. He said a lot of wonderful things, such as not being able to live without me and hoping that I would want to live with him and marry him someday. He ended his loving speech with his ex-girlfriend's name instead of mine. FML

Today, I was babysitting a really annoying kid who threw his food all over the kitchen, so I gave him a time-out. When his mother came home, he ran to her and said, "Mommy, it's not true what you told me, fat people are NOT nice!" FML

Today, I managed to pop my blouse open by pressing against it with my chest. What's less sexy is that I can also do this with my belly. FML

Today, while driving, I hit a parked car. Trying to be clever, I stuck a note to the windshield and wrote, "People think I'm leaving you my details, but nope. Tough luck!" I realized later on that the note was my business card. FML

Today, I called my gynecologist to tell him about some intimate issues. Only after describing them in detail did the guy tell me I had the wrong number. FML

SWITZERLAND

Today, it was election day for student council president. I decided to be nice and vote for my only competitor because it was her birthday. I lost by one vote. FML

Today, I was having sex with my girlfriend. Things were getting pretty hot, so I decided to smack her butt. I missed and smacked my balls instead. Real hard. FML

Today, I worked up the courage to comment on my crush's Facebook profile photo. I wrote, "Cool picture." Later, I logged on and saw that he had replied: "Who the fuck are you?" FML

Today, I reached for my beer and took a huge swallow before I realized that I had picked up my friend's tobacco spit cup. "Vomit" is not a strong enough word to describe what happened next. FML

CROATIA

Today, my boyfriend and I were at a restaurant with a few other couples, and my boyfriend started to rant about how "all the hot chicks are dumb." Apparently, I'm either ugly or stupid. FML

LATVIA

Today, I stumbled upon my girlfriend's Twitter account, which I didn't know existed. A recent entry states that living with me is pathetic: "It's just that the current economical situation doesn't leave me with many options." FML

UNITED KINGDOM

Today, I saw a video of me last night, hammered, climbing my wardrobe, screaming, "I WANT TO GO TO NARNIA," naked. FML

Today, my boyfriend of two years took me to get a tattoo with his name on it. He paid for it. After it was done, he told me it was over between us and he thought it'd be a nice reminder of him. FML

Today, I found out just how thin the walls at my new dorm building are. It turns out I can hear the creepy guy next door say my full name over and over again very slowly while pleasuring himself. FML

Today, I got a call saying that my son was chasing all the girls in the class with his "Sword of Death" (my dildo). FML

Today, I had to pretend to give birth in a play. I wanted to make it as realistic as possible but ended up crapping myself onstage by accident. FML

Today, my five-year-old sister informed me she had left me a present on my bed. She had tied a ribbon around a dead rat's neck and propped it up on my pillow. The label says his name was Bert. FML

Today, my boyfriend and I were starting to get in the mood. I get on top of him, lean down to kiss him, and he begins to laugh. Puzzled, I ask him why. He tells me that when I'm naked and on top of him, I remind him of a cow, with "udders." Offended, I go to get off. "No, no," he protests, "a SEXY cow." FML

Today, I repaired a boiler for a wealthy guy in a big house. While there, I fixed a leaking tap for free. When I went to go, the man slipped something into my shirt pocket and said, "Have a drink on me." When I got to my truck, I discovered that he'd given me a tea bag. FML

Today, my mom grounded me for going to my boyfriend's house instead of the library. She said my boyfriend's mom phoned up because she could hear us getting it on in his room. The thing is, I did go to the library. FML

Today, for our one-year anniversary, my boyfriend decided to make me a patchwork blanket. The thing is, the patches were stains from bedsheets from where the "wet spot" was. He thought it was romantic. FML

Today, I was the paramedic at the scene of a car accident. One lady was hurt, and we had trouble getting any information from her as she was sobbing. I radioed in the details and said, "A lady in her mid-30s, ETA 10 minutes." She stopped crying, slapped me, and said, "I'm 28." FML

Today, I was in the cafeteria when I noticed a new worker cleaning a table. As I passed her, she looked up and smiled at me. Thinking she was pulling a funny face, I jokingly crossed my eyes and smiled back. Later, she served me my lunch, and I could see that she was actually cross-eyed. FML

Today, I had a terrible stomach bug. I quickly jumped off the toilet and crouched over the bowl. I vomited with such force that I splashed the water back into my face. FML

Today, I was talking to my boyfriend while driving to meet him. While chatting, I told him that I had a rip in my favorite jeans. When he sympathetically apologized, I said, "It's okay, you're just going to take them off in a minute anyway." I forgot my mom was in the car. FML

Today, I found out that my boss plays a trick on all the interns. He calls you to his office, then leaves you waiting outside until you get annoyed and leave. Apparently, the old record was 45 minutes. I waited four hours. FML

Today, my boyfriend broke up with me, by text, while we were in the same room. FML

Today, I was playing songs at a funeral in my church. As the organ wasn't in tune, I had to use an electronic piano instead. All was going well until, at the end of a speech, I accidentally hit the "demo" button. None of the grieving relatives were impressed by my drumbeats and turntable scratches. FML

Today, I was home alone and decided to do some naked cleaning just because I could. After half an hour of liberating naked-dusting, I turned around to see my boyfriend and his best friend gaping at me openmouthed. His older brother, however, gave a creepy smile and a thumbs-up. FML

Today, I woke up crying in the middle of a nightmare in which my boyfriend of eight months shot me through the heart while laughing as I screamed, "I love you!" After I told him about this, he took me into his arms as I cried, stroked my back, and said, "What kind of gun was it?" FML

Today, I was on webcam with someone and the conversation fizzled, so I said, "brb." I sat there for five minutes, not realizing I had left my webcam on. FML

Today, I arranged the food on my plate in a smiley face in an attempt to make myself feel better. I'm a 38-year-old man. It worked. FML

Today, I was reading a text from my girlfriend while I was on line at the supermarket. As I was thinking of what to reply, the cashier handed me my change. I got confused and said, "Thank you, I love you!" FML

Today, I had a big exam. Twenty minutes in, I could feel people turning around and looking at me. I ignored them at first, but toward the one-hour mark it got more distracting. I stood up and yelled, "Why is everyone staring at me?" Turns out I was seated directly in front of the clock. FML

Today, I met my new roommate. I also met her stuffed animals, who introduced themselves to me. My roommate makes inanimate objects talk. FML

Today, I had to pull cheese out of my PS3's disc tray because my younger brother assumed all PS3s could grill stuff because "YouTube told him." FML

Today, I was hanging out with a guy I liked. We sat in the gardens, me facing the path, him with his back to it. We were in deep conversation when I noticed a dog that looked exactly like mine. Then I looked up and saw a man that looked like my dad. Yes—my parents followed me on a date. FML

Today, I was having a nice moment with my young granddaughter. She was affectionately stroking my face, and we were both quite content, until she said, "Aw, Grandma, your skin feels just like a crocodile." FML

Today, I got my first acting part. I played the role of a bad boy who has to grab the ass of the leading lady, who then slaps me in the face. The ass grab was done in one take. The slap required 14. FML

Today, I was helping a friend redecorate. Her dad had put up some shelving that we presumed was stable. It broke, and all the expensive vases and collectibles fell to the floor. On instinct, I leapt forward to catch the closest thing. It was not an expensive vase. It was a cactus. FML

Today, I received an email from the girls at work. It was an invite to lunch that ended by saying, "PLEASE don't tell Francoise, I don't think any of us can take any more of her!" I am Francoise. FML

Today, I got out of bed and immediately went to the window, as it was supposed to snow. I saw a man walking his dog and he waved at me. I waved back enthusiastically and realized I was naked. FML

Today, I posted a picture of my boyfriend and me kissing on Facebook. He untagged himself. FML

Today, I wore a beautiful new dress that I got for only $5 in a sale. I've been turning heads in it all day. When I got home, my mum pulled the massive red $5 tag off the back. FML

Today, I was walking while texting. I thought I was going in a straight line but I ended up walking right into an open phone booth. A woman was inside making a phone call. I lost my balance, pinning her up against the wall. She thought I was attacking her and clobbered me with the receiver. FML

Today, my boyfriend of five years sent me a letter for my birthday. He'd forgotten to put a stamp on it, so I had to pay to get it. There was a letter telling me he'd found someone else. I payed for my own breakup letter. FML

Today, my boyfriend texted me telling me how much he loved me, and that he wanted my virginity. We have already done it. I don't think he meant to send that text to me. FML

Today, I found out my boyfriend keeps a gun under his pillow. This was only after my friends and I surprised him with his birthday cake while he was sleeping. FML

Today, good news! The guitar I have been saving up for, for five months, finally arrived. It came in a beautiful black-and-white case, which is impossible to get into without a key. They didn't pack the key. FML

Today, for the third time this week, my boss made me switch desks. Each new desk is closer to the door than the last one. I think he's trying to tell me something. FML

Today, I was on webcam to my girlfriend, who was naked. She turned the webcam to point to the screen for a second and I could see that she was also on webcam with another guy. FML

Today, I woke to find my husband holding my hand. I smiled at him and asked if he was all right. Apparently, I snore less if he touches me. FML

Today, I found out that my ex-husband just had a baby with his new partner. We only split up a week ago. FML

Today, I finally got up the guts to tell a co-worker that I have feelings for him and asked him if he would like to go out sometime after work. He politely declined, and I wasn't too hurt. That was until I heard him tell another coworker that he doesn't "do fat chicks." FML

Today, I went to my best friend's wedding. All my friends and their boyfriends were seated at one table, while I, as the only single girl in the group, was put on a table with all the other single people. They were all more than 40 years older than me. I feel like I have seen my future. FML

Today, my boyfriend was getting his guitar off his wall. He accidentally dropped it, and it fell straight on my head. I pretended I didn't see him quickly check the guitar over for damage before he started apologizing. FML

SOUTH
AMERICA

PERU

Today, I was surfing. I saw a cop writing a ticket for my car, so I swam as fast as I could to stop him. I got caught in a wave and smashed onto the rocks. I ended up with a huge, bleeding scratch on my back, a broken surfboard, and a note saying that I had a flat tire. FML

ECUADOR

Today, I really had to use the airplane lavatory, and afterward the flight attendants continuously sprayed air freshener for 10 minutes. FML

BRAZIL

Today, I was making out with my boyfriend and he tried to put his hand inside my pants. I didn't want it to be that easy so I denied, but he insisted a lot and I finally let him. He started to sing "We Are the Champions." FML

Today, the gas station right in front of my apartment had people listening to loud music all night. I had a three-hour test at 7:30 a.m. and didn't get any sleep. Worst of all, here in Brazil, calling the police won't help a thing. Instead of breaking up the party, they'll stop by and join it. FML

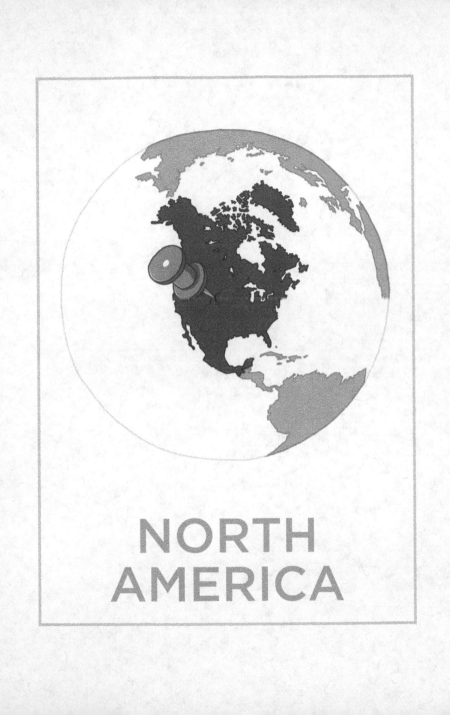

NORTH
AMERICA

CANADA

Today, I was serving a family at the restaurant where I work. When I went to ask the little girl what she wanted, I was tongue-tied and got "cutie" and "hun" mixed up and ended up asking: "What can I get for you, cuntie?" FML

Today, I went up to a secluded mountain my boyfriend took me to for our first date. As I saw another couple hooking up in the bushes, I phoned my boyfriend to tell him someone found our secret spot. His Bob Marley ringtone started playing from the bush. FML

Today, I found out that my sister who is 16 years older than me is actually my biological mother. She and my parents decided it was best that I didn't know who my real mother was, and for me to be raised by my grandparents as their child. I've always hated my sister. FML

Today, half asleep, I dropped my pill before I could take it. I quickly picked it up and washed it down. Five hours later, I found my pill on the ground. What did I swallow? FML

Today, I noticed I have to lift up my fat to see my penis. FML

Today, I was watching this TV show where a man was describing how much he loved this woman, how he made every opportunity to see her, and how he loved her in a way nobody else could. I smiled, because that's exactly the way I feel about my crush. Then I realized the program was about stalkers. FML

Today, I finally told my parents I would be changing bedrooms because I could no longer stand hearing them having sex, which is awkward and disturbing. Later, my dad came and asked me quietly if I thought my mom sounded "satisfied." FML

Today, I was fingering my girlfriend. When suddenly she started crying at the peak of her orgasm, and I asked what was wrong, she replied, "I-I-I MISS HIM!" She was crying about her ex-boyfriend. FML

Today, I went on a blind date. We had agreed on meeting in front of a park. Thinking I was there first, I texted her, "I'm already there, sitting next to the heavy chick." I heard a beep. SHE was the "heavy chick." FML

Today, I went for a jog. While I passed by my neighbor's house, their six-year-old son started throwing peanuts at me, screaming, "I hope this kills you!" because I'm allergic to peanuts. FML

Today, I was at my boss's house for a company barbecue. Earlier I had taken muscle relaxants to calm my lower back pain. After a few drinks, it was clear the alcohol and medication do not mix. I woke up a few hours later to find out I had stripped naked and jumped into the four-foot cake before passing out. FML

Today, I was volunteering at a zoo event for special-needs kids. My job was to dress up in a kangaroo costume and greet them. One kid came up and said, "You're not real!" and kicked me in the nuts. FML

Today, it was my girlfriend's birthday. To surprise her, I told her that I was going away on business and could not be there on her birthday. When I showed up at her house to surprise her with a present and cake, she opened the door in her underwear, beside a man in his boxers. She was surprised. FML

Today, I learned that when blender jars aren't locked, they fly off the blender, into the air, hit you in the head, and explode all over your kitchen. Today, I also learned that after I'm attacked by a flying blender, the first thing my boyfriend asks is if I'm still gonna make him a smoothie. FML

Today, I came home from work and went to open the door. I looked in the window and saw a man in my house. Terrified, I called the police. They came, searched the house, and found nothing missing. I went back inside and looked through the window and saw him again. It was my reflection. FML

Today, my boyfriend of three months and I were in the middle of a heavy make-out session when his cell rang. Normally, he'd ignore it. This time, however, he pushed me off of him and said, "Shit! It's probably my girlfriend!" I thought I was his girlfriend. FML

Today, I found out that my parents are first cousins. FML

Today, in math class, we were learning about gravity. To demonstrate, my teacher asked me to stand on the desk and then step off. As I stepped on it, the desk curved inward and cracked. Everyone was dying of laughter. F gravity. FML

Today, I was getting ready for my first date with a boy I really like when my dad insisted on meeting him. My dad is super protective and a cop. He cleaned his gun in front of my date and made it clear he had to be careful with me. My date started to cry when we got to the car. FML

Today, I was walking to a Halloween party wearing a zombie costume. Apparently, my delusional neighbor found the costume too realistic. He tackled me. FML

Today, I was riding my bike on the side of the road because there was no sidewalk. Then a car with a loud horn honked at me. Pissed off, I turned around and screamed, "Shut the fuck up!" It was my girlfriend's parents saying hi. FML

Today, I was supposed to catch a flight to New York. My five-year-old son handed me my carry-on bag as I left the house. Turns out he had put his older brother's BB gun into my bag to "keep me safe." I missed my flight after I was detained and strip-searched. FML

Today, I was straightening my hair when I heard this crunching, sizzling sound. Taking the flat iron away, I realized that I had just fused a spider to my hair. FML

Today, I woke up from a nap on my new bed to see my phone lit up with new texts. My roommate sent out "Wanna test out my new bed?" as a mass text while I was asleep to every boy in my phone. Mark will be here in an hour. Jon wants to know what I'm wearing. FML

Today, after practicing a song for my girlfriend on guitar all day, I invited her over to my house to play it for her. After a long speech about how this was for her, I proceeded to play for about three seconds when I broke a string, which slapped her in her face. FML

Today, none of my 500 Facebook friends responded to my status about "Who wants to hang out during summer holidays?" I proceeded to create an imaginary person on a different account to respond and ask me to hang out with him. I had a conversation on FB with myself. FML

Today, I realized that my plug-in air freshener lasts longer than any of my relationships have. FML

Today, at my grandmother's funeral, we had to sing. My dad is a horrible singer, and I tried my hardest not to laugh. I turned red, and tears were falling from my eyes. My stepmother held my hand and said that she was in a better place. I couldn't hold it any longer. I laughed my ass off. FML

Today, at my job as a cashier, a man and his three-year-old son got in line. The father said, "Give this to the pretty lady," looking at me. The kid looked at me, looked at his dad, and walked over to the next cashier. FML

Today, driving some friends back from a party, I said, "Did everyone see Lisa totally hanging off of Pat tonight?! It was hilarious!!" There was a long silence, then one of my friends said, "You know Lisa is in the car, right?" FML

Today, I paid $80 to change my cell number because my ex-girlfriend had been stalking me. To inform all of my friends of the change, I sent a mass text message to everyone in my phone book. Including my ex. FML

Today, I got into a heated argument with the guy I'm seeing because he refused to let me pick up the check at dinner. I thought it was sexist. When he finally agreed, I gave the waiter my credit card, only to have him return a minute later telling me it was declined. FML

Today, my boyfriend's head was on my lap. I bent down to kiss him. My stomach rolls got there first. FML

Today, my parents told me that I was born to entertain my brother. I guess my life has a purpose. FML

Today, I was explaining to my four-year-old daughter that we have to wait until the sign says "walk" before crossing the street and stop if it says "don't walk." When we were halfway across the intersection, the light changed. She refused to budge. I had to drag her in front of the amused-looking motorists. FML

Today, I realized that when my boyfriend said, "I'll love you forever," what he really meant was, "I'll love you until I meet your significantly more attractive sister." FML

Today, I had to get an ultrasound, which required me to drink three glasses of water beforehand. The doctor said I had too much and told me to go pee out just a little and come back. It took a lot of effort to hold the rest in. The first thing she did when I got back was press on my abdomen. I peed myself. FML

Today, I was excited about showing everyone at work my new piercing. It's in an unusual place in my ear. Before I had the chance to tell anyone about it, someone asked, "Are you wearing a hearing aid?" FML

Today, my girlfriend and I were getting it on when her cat attacked me. I was pissed, so I grabbed the cat and rushed outside to get rid of it. Little did I know, her parents were home, sitting outside. So I was naked, with a feral cat trying to kill me. All I could say was, "Nice weather?" FML

Today, I was on my bed on top of my boyfriend when I lost my balance and fell. My father walked in the door to see what the noise was. I don't know what is more embarrassing, my father walking in, or him walking in saying, "That's an expensive bed." FML

Today, I was feeling ill after a severe anxiety attack. I asked my boyfriend to hold my hand until I fell asleep. He said he couldn't because he needed both hands to play on his Game Boy. FML

Today, my dad screamed at me, called me a monster, told me he wanted me to move out. Why? I slammed the microwave door. FML

Today, my mom decided our whole family is going on a diet. The vet had told her that our dog is overweight, and she didn't "want Twix to suffer alone." FML

Today, my boyfriend and I had sex for the first time in months. His apology took longer than the sex did. FML

Today, I went to my girlfriend's house. She had promised me we'd get it on. Instead, I got a list of reasons why I make her depressed. FML

Today, I was video chatting with my girlfriend. I screen-copied my desktop to show her the conversation I was having with my best friend. She replied asking why I had a porn site open on the other tab. FML

Today, I decided to clean my room, find a job, and ask a girl on a date. I ended up playing video games on-line. FML

USA

Today, I came home to find a sock I'd previously used to whack off on my bed with googly eyes and a mouth drawn on it, with a note that read, "Because you can't find a real girl, I made your current one prettier. Love Mom." FML

Today, I went on a date with a guy for the first time. We talked for a while, and we were having a good time. Suddenly, he put his hand on my stomach and said, "Soon, this will be plump with my seed." FML

Today, I took the bus to work and a sweet old lady sat down next to me. Halfway to work, she fell asleep and her head was on my shoulder. Trying to be nice, I gently tried to wake her up before my stop came. She wasn't sleeping. I let a dead woman lie on me for 30 minutes. FML

Today, I had a very intense sexual dream that left me panting when I woke up. It was the best orgasm I'd ever had. The trouble was, it wasn't about a hot girl or anything sexy. It was about bacon. FML

Today, my husband of nine years announced he was gay. He insinuated that he was only able to achieve erections because I looked like a man. FML

Today, while at the Golden Gate Bridge, I spotted a large group of Asians trying to take a picture. Trying to be a diplomat, I slowly say, "You . . . want me . . . take picture?" while using hand motions. The man looks at me and says, "No thanks, asshole, I got it," in plain English. FML

Today, I was taking a nap. Apparently, my two-year-old daughter decided to crawl on top of the covers on my bed because she heard thunder and got scared. I thought she was one of our cats so I kicked her off. She hit the wall. FML

Today, my boyfriend and I were fooling around. All of a sudden, we heard "Pop Goes the Weasel" outside my window. My boyfriend excitedly says, "ICE CREAM MAN!" and proceeds to flip me over, grab his clothes, and run out of my room. FML

Today, I was getting sick of listening to the guy in the next room over getting nasty with some girl, so I called my girlfriend to see if she wanted to go get some food. Then I heard her phone ring. Through the wall. FML

Today, my dog started to hump my leg. He always does this and I heard that humping in the dog world meant dominance. Well, I decided to instill my dominance, so I dry-humped him back. As I was doing this, I said, "How do you like that!" Then my mom walked in. FML

Today, it's my eighteenth birthday. My parents got me a $5 gift certificate to iTunes. It came for free with the iPhone they just bought my sister for her middle school graduation. FML

Today, my friend took my cat to be put down because he has a tumor and I couldn't bear to take him myself. I have two cats. She took the wrong one. FML

Today, my tampon string was hanging from my bathing suit. My boyfriend thought it was a thread hanging from my bikini bottom. He publicly pulled out my tampon. FML

Today, I ran over a squirrel. I saw it twitching so I backed over it to end its suffering. It wasn't a squirrel, it was a kitten. The children it belonged to watched as I ran over their kitten. TWICE. FML

Today, I found out my boyfriend stacks things on me while I sleep. Apparently, his record is four pillows, a textbook, and the cat. FML

Today, I had my first job interview and didn't have much of an appetite because of nerves. So I grabbed a brownie that my roommate had left in the fridge and ate it on the train ride into the city. About 20 minutes into my interview, I was so stoned I couldn't speak. FML

Today, I was at my girlfriend's house. Things began to get heated and we started doing it on the living room couch. Near the end I decided to whisper in her ear, "Who's your daddy?" I heard behind me, "I am." FML

Today, I found out that the girl I've been dating online for over a year is actually a very bored 14-year-old boy. FML

Today, I went to the store to buy groceries. I didn't care how I looked, so I wore an old T-shirt that said, "Thousands of my potential children died on your daughter's face last night." I ran into my girlfriend's parents at the store. FML

Today, I was on my way home when I saw a cop hiding behind a Budget truck. I immediately slowed down and prayed that he wouldn't give me a ticket. Then I realized I was walking. FML

Today, I was at the gym when someone came up behind me and shouted in my ear, scaring the living shit out of me. I jumped into a karate pose in front of everyone. No one was behind me. It was a new song starting on my headphones. FML

Today, my boyfriend and I were fooling around. It started to get hot and he took out his penis for the first time. This was the first one I've seen in real life so I decided I'd compliment it. I had no idea what to say so I said, "It's pretty." FML

Today, I witnessed a serious car accident and was interviewed by the local news. During the interview, I said, "It was terrible. It was like watching a silent movie . . . but there was sound!" The interview has been aired six times. FML

Today, I was at the mall blasting music on my iPod, which was in the breast pocket of my shirt. I noticed a cute girl smiling at me so I started to walk over while turning down the volume. It looked like I was rubbing my nipple. FML

Today, it's my birthday. I've gotten three calls all day. The first one was my fiancé, saying he wanted the ring back. The second was my best friend, confessing that she had been sleeping with my fiancé for the past three months. The third was the dentist's office, singing me a happy birthday. FML

Today, for the first time ever, a woman saw my penis. I am 30 years old. The woman was my doctor. She snorted to cover a laugh and apologized. FML

Today, I went to meet my girlfriend's parents for the first time. I accidentally drove past their house the first time but saw the whole family outside waiting to meet me. I pulled a U-turn and heard a thud. The whole family watched me run over their dog. FML

Today, I was picking my daughter up at day care. She was outside playing kickball. A red ball rolled over to me, and, trying to impress the kids, I kicked it back. I turned around to see three crying six-year-olds. It was their hamster. FML

Today, my adorable eight-year-old son told me he no longer wanted me to pick him up from school. When I asked why, he said, "I told everyone at school my mommy is pretty . . ." FML

Today, I was at the mall with my mom. She was pissing me off, so I started screaming at her and causing a scene. I ended up falling all the way down the up escalator. People applauded. FML

Today, while I was taking a shower, a dime fell on my foot. The only place it could have come from? One of my fat rolls. FML

Today, while I was running on the treadmill at the gym, the girl next to me slipped and went flying back against the wall. Indecisive whether to get off and help her or to just keep going, I lost my focus and footing and flew back next to her. FML

Today, I met my girlfriend's very religious parents for the first time for dinner. Somehow we got to talking about her groin hernias that were repaired as a baby. I never knew she had hernias repaired and said, "But she doesn't have any scars down there." Long awkward silence. FML

Today, the dentist sneezed in my mouth. FML

Today, while walking in the mall, I noticed two people rush past me in wheelchairs. Thinking they were racing, I started rooting for the guy who was ahead. Turns out his wheelchair was malfunctioning and the other was chasing after to help. He then crashed into a water fountain and fell in. FML

Today, my boyfriend returned from a two-month internship in New York. As I saw him exit the plane, I imagined him kissing me passionately and spinning me around like in movies. As I opened my arms to embrace him, he ran past me, saying, "BRB, I GOTTA TAKE A SHIT." FML

Today, it was my wedding day, and while I was standing next to my husband in front of all of our guests, I was rocking on my heels because I was nervous. I rocked too far and fell backward. My husband didn't come to help me up. He just said at the top of his lungs, "FAIL!" FML

Today, my five-year-old son told me that when he grows up he's going to be my boyfriend. I thought it was kind of cute until I asked him why. "Because you need one." FML

Today, my boyfriend and I took a late-night drive, and after a while he stopped at a gas station and asked if I wanted anything. I replied, "Guess." He came out and gave me a box of tampons. Apparently, I've been bitchy. FML

Today, I told my parents that I was going out with my boyfriend and they agreed to let me go as long as I was home by midnight. Did I come home on time? Yes. Was my shirt right side out? No. FML

Today, a woman drove through my house. She was texting and eating watermelon at the same time. I didn't know that was even possible to do. FML

Today, my daughter had just left for a date with her boyfriend. All of a sudden, she runs back in the house, screaming, "I forgot to take my birth control!" That is not something a father wants to hear. FML

Today, I got up the nerve to text the girl I've had a crush on to ask her on a date. I got back "Error message 3265: Number No Longer In Swrvice." "Service" was spelled wrong. When I looked it up, I learned that error message 3265 does not exist. FML

Today, I bought a new mailbox to replace the old one that was stolen. Two hours after I put the new mailbox up, the old one was back and the new one was missing. FML

Today, my girlfriend of eight years dumped me. When I asked if there was another guy, she responded, "You were the other guy." FML

Today, I was coaching a little league soccer game. I was telling one of my players to go cover another kid. I said, "Go cover the little yellow kid!" because he happened to be wearing a yellow shirt. He also happened to be Asian. I then got death stares from his family members. FML

Today, I found out that my dad hides his Viagra from my mom by keeping it in an aspirin container. Now I have a terrible headache and a boner. FML

Today, I was in a tour group going through a cave and our guide stopped, turned off the lights, and told us to be quiet so we could feel absolute silence. I farted. FML

Today, my wife changed her Facebook status from "married" to "widowed." I'm scared. FML

Today, I found a bell that had been tied into the tassel of my ski hat by my twin sister as part of a long-standing prank war between us. I'm deaf and have apparently been jingling like an elf for over a week. FML

Today, my friend was pulled over and told to get out of the car. The officer motioned for me to get out of the car, too, so I reached behind me to get my shoes. He then pointed his gun at my face and frantically asked my friend if I had a gun. My friend calmly replied, "No, but shoot him anyway." FML

Today, while I was in the middle of having sex with my husband, instead of saying something sexy in my ear, he whispered, "We are so gonna make pizza after this!" FML

Today, I finally got Wii Fit to lose some weight. Came home and set it all up, only to be told that I weigh too much to use the board. FML

Today, I sprained my wrist playing Guitar Hero. The ER doctor called all of his coworkers in to hear my story. They all laughed. FML

Today, I got pulled over while dancing to crazy techno beats in the car. The officer RAN out of his car and up to mine and pounded on my window. He thought I was having a seizure. FML

Today, we were visiting my great-grandma, who has Alzheimer's. We spent most of the day with her and she didn't know who we all were. When it was time for us to leave, I gave her a hug good-bye, and she whispered into my ear, "You're my type." FML

Today, while talking to my boyfriend, I was frantically searching for my cell phone. He was curious as to what I was doing so I told him. There was a long silence followed by laughter. He could hardly breathe as he told me, "Honey, you're on your phone talking to me." FML

Today, I went to the pool. When I hit the water, the top of my swimsuit came off. I tried to put it on underwater, and the lifeguard thought I was drowning. He pulled me out in front of everyone. Topless. FML

Today, I was home on leave and having breakfast with my parents and my younger brothers. I guess I got too used to the rougher language around the Army barracks where I'm stationed. At the breakfast table I asked my mom to "pass me the F*ing butter." FML

Today, a Milk-Bone commercial came on TV. At the end of the commercial, they whistle and throw a Milk-Bone across the screen, prompting my 100-pound German shepherd to leap off the couch and pummel my brand-new plasma-screen TV. FML

Today, I was volunteering at a school. There's this really bratty boy there and he was being rude, so I joked, "How are you ever gonna get a girlfriend when you're so mean?" He responded, "I think the better question is, how are you ever gonna get a boyfriend when you're so ugly?" He's seven. FML

Today, my boyfriend of five years gave me the silent treatment, refusing to talk to me or do anything more than glare at me during the entire three-hour drive we took this morning. Why? Because I slept with his best friend. In his dream last night. FML

Today, I was in a public restroom when the girl in the stall next to me started asking me how I was doing. Thinking it was weird but not wanting to be rude, I answered her questions. Halfway through our conversation, she said: "Hold on, the girl in the stall next to me thinks I'm talking to her." FML

Today, when my girlfriend and I were exchanging some naughty pictures, I accidentally sent one to all of my contacts, including my ex, my boss, and even Pizza Hut. FML

Today, I found out that my husband made a replica of our family on The Sims 3. I also found out he killed me off a couple weeks ago and made a new wife, KiKi. FML

Today, my boyfriend picked me up to come spend the night at his house, and on the way he started pulling over to get some condoms. I told him no need, I was on my period. He turned the car around and took me home. FML

Today, my family threw me a surprise party. I was so surprised I punched my mom in the face when she screamed, "SURPRISE!" FML

Today, I met my girlfriend's parents for the first time. We got on the discussion of animals, and I showed them a picture of my cat on my phone. Being a touch screen, when her father grabbed it, it changed the picture. To a picture of my girlfriend, fully nude. FML

Today, my mother found condoms in my room. She asked why and I said, "Just in case." She started laughing hysterically. FML

Today, my parents booked my 18th birthday party at Chuck E. Cheese's. FML

Today, I was having sex with my girlfriend. She started panting harder and going, "AH, AH, AH . . ." and I thought she was about to come. Next thing I know, there's snot splattered all over my face and neck. Turns out it was a sneeze. FML

Today, my boyfriend proposed by sending me a bumper sticker on Facebook that said, "Bitch, let's get married." FML

Today, I went to a concert. They had a feature where you could send a picture of something from your cell phone and they'd put it on the big screens, so I sent a picture of myself. When the picture came up on the screens, the entire crowd went, "Ewwww!" FML

Today, I realized that my company's calendar is synchronized throughout the whole building. The entire company knows that I had sex with my wife last Wednesday and Friday. FML

Today, I received a signed vintage Beatles album from my wife for my birthday. It's the same album some jerk way overbid me for on eBay. That jerk was my wife, using my credit card. FML

Today, I decided to start working out because my friends said I'm scrawny and weak. I bought a big, expensive container of protein powder to take before working out. I wasn't strong enough to open the lid. FML

Today, I was pulled over for speeding. The cop was hot so I flirted with him as much as I could. But when he came back to the car, he still gave me a ticket. Feeling desperate, I said, "I thought you didn't give tickets to pretty girls." His response: "We don't." FML

Today, I was at the gynecologist for a routine checkup. The doctor was new, and I was just slightly uncomfortable with him. About mid-checkup, as he felt around my uterus, he said in a cartoonish voice, "Oh, it's so squishy up here." The doctor turned me into a sock puppet. FML

Today, I made a bowl of spaghetti for me and my girlfriend. I tried that move from *Lady and the Tramp* where the boy and the girl both slurp the same piece of spaghetti and end up kissing. Only when I tried it, my spaghetti went down too far in my throat and I ended up coughing it up on her. FML

Today, I brought my lunch to work in the only box I had lying around my apartment—a small one from FedEx. When I went to the bathroom before lunch, I returned to my desk to find that one of my coworkers had mailed my lunch back to my apartment. FML

Today, I was on line at the grocery store with my three-year-old son. He was holding a container of yogurt that had a cow wearing sunglasses on it. He shouted, "Mommy, look at the fat cow with the sunglasses on!" To my horror, the obese woman in front of us turned around. She was wearing sunglasses. FML

Today, my rescue squad unit responded to a 911 call from a woman who felt like she was going to pass out. We knocked on her locked door a couple of times with no answer. Fearing she might be unconscious, I kicked in the door. She was about to open it and passed out from the concussion I gave her. FML

Today, I was on a roller coaster, and the 13-year-old sitting next to me was completely terrified. To cheer him up, I threw my hands in the air. While my hands were up, we hit a curve and I elbowed him in the face, making him cry. FML

Today, I was getting a checkup, and the doctor asked me: "Have you been having any intimate relations?" The first thing I blurted out was: "You mean with other people?" FML

Today, I had to retake an hour-long MRI scan because I got an erection midway through. FML

Today, I discovered that my cleaning lady steals valuables from me and covers it up by saying that "the vacuum must've eaten it." FML

Today, I finally got around to organizing my closet. Discarded clothes fell into three distinct categories: Too Small, Yellow Pits, Stained with Food. FML

Today, I held the door open for an old man in a motorized wheelchair. He missed the door, ran over my foot, and called me an asshole for getting in his way. FML

Today, I have to pack for tomorrow's family vacation. For one week I get to be stuck in a one-bedroom cabin with my alcoholic father, bipolar mother, and two much-younger siblings, who have a passion for screaming. FML

Today, after I had a large, dramatic fight with my girlfriend in a parking lot, we stopped arguing altogether and hugged, dropping the issue. Twenty seconds later, I accidentally slammed her hand in the car door, breaking two of her fingers. FML

Today, I went horseback riding. Somebody yelled something behind me, so I turned around. Next thing I knew, I was on the ground and my head was killing me. It turns out I ran into a tree branch. The person behind me had been saying, "Watch out." FML

Today, I fell asleep on the couch and must have rolled off. When I woke up on the floor, my braces were stuck to the rug. My mom had to cut me loose with scissors. FML

Today, I was relaxing on the couch after a long day with my annoying aunt when I heard my sister come in from the garage. I loudly asked, "Do you think Aunt Stacy knows everybody doesn't like her?" It wasn't my sister. It was my aunt returning the purse I had left in her car. FML

Today, my boyfriend's mother screamed at me for half an hour, calling me a slut because she found a black lacy thong in my boyfriend's bed. I didn't have the heart to tell her it wasn't mine. FML

Today, I got called a "loser" by an old man wearing pink flip-flops and riding a purple moped. FML

Today, I found out that while getting your hair cut, you should say yes or no instead of nodding your head. FML

Today, I was making out with my new boyfriend when he pulled away and looked deep into my eyes. He smiled and said, "I don't care what anyone else says, I think you're beautiful." FML

Today, I was late to work because the train broke down. Yesterday, I was late because the train in front of me broke down. The week before that, I was late because the SWAT team shut the entire train station down. Even the interns think I'm making this up. FML

Today, I was studying late and kept hearing weird screeching sounds from outside. I couldn't figure out what it was and started getting really freaked-out. It wasn't until later that I realized it was just my nose whistling. FML

Today, my aunt and I wanted to do something nice, so we made cookies for a local nursing home. Nobody ate them. FML

Today, I called my mother to check up on her. Lately, she's been having some financial problems, so last week I sent her my last $100 to help her out until her next paycheck. She said she used the money to euthanize the family dog. FML

Today, I bought a used car from a friend. After getting the car home and inspecting it further, I found one of my wife's earrings in the backseat. FML

Today, I asked my boyfriend if I looked all right for our date. He said, "Honey, you look fine, just don't go out in public like that." FML

Today, my youngest son thought that Red Bull actually gave him wings. What it actually gave him was a trip to the ER and seven stitches. It also gave me a meeting with social services. FML

Today, I was eating lunch with my boyfriend when I started choking. My boyfriend took it as an opportunity to sneak food off my plate. FML

Today, it was the third day of a camping trip with my "friends." I woke up in my boxers with my hand glued to my forehead. FML

Today, after several hours of trying to get my triplet daughters to go to bed, they finally fell asleep. Exhausted, I went to the bathroom so I could get ready for bed. Without thinking about it, I dropped the toilet seat down rather loudly and flushed the toilet. All three girls woke up crying. FML

Today, in math class, I had the urge to fart. I had the bright idea that if I dropped my textbook and farted at the same time, nobody would hear it. I dropped my textbook, everyone looked at me, then I farted. Loudly. FML

Today, I finally met the guy I've been talking to online for a year. In my profile, I had dropped 10 pounds off my real weight. He had shaved 20 years off his age. FML

Today, my boyfriend moved. I found out when I went over to surprise him with take-out food and he was pulling out of the driveway. He flipped me off as he drove past. FML

Today, I finally got my first kiss. I was so excited, I pissed myself. FML

Today, I spent a long time steam-cleaning a mystery stain on my living room carpet. I turned the light on to get a better look at it, and realized that it was a shadow. FML

Today, I was on an airplane and had to go to the bathroom. The guy next to me was asleep and blocking the aisle. I tapped him on the shoulder, and he responded by punching me in the stomach. FML

Today, my math teacher told me to learn how to say, "Welcome to Walmart." FML

Today, I learned that you should never, under any circumstance, take a laxative and a sleeping pill on the same night. FML

Today, after I broke up with my boyfriend, some of my friends decided to take me to a comedy club for a girls' night. My friend's jealous husband decided he had to come along, then decided to invite my other friends' boyfriends. I ended up being the seventh wheel on a night meant to cheer me up. FML

Today, I was taking my dog for a walk when two younger-looking boys rode their bikes up toward me. One said, "What about her?" The other boy said, "Nah, she's ugly." FML

Today, my roommate came out of the bathroom, tossed a *Playboy* on the coffee table, threw away a used condom, dug his hand into my bag of Doritos, and washed his hands. In that order. FML

Today, I finally weighed myself after going on a strict diet of only fruits, vegetables, and coffee. I had gained weight. FML

Today, I'm three months pregnant. Hours after the father of my baby bought me a wedding ring, he decided to get drunk and tell me that he doesn't see himself with me for the rest of his life and doesn't really want to get married. Oh, and he hates my dog. FML

Today, I got a bird as a pet. I thought it would be funny to put it on my head and take a picture. When the flash went off, the bird flew off my head and pooped at the same time. You can see it in the picture. FML

Today, my husband purposefully said something to upset me. When I asked why he would do that, he told me it was to test my Prozac. FML

Today, my kitten decided that having diarrhea was not a good enough reason to stop running in circles around my living room. FML

Today, my dad decided that my diploma makes a good pen-tester. FML

Today, I had to drive 300 miles to a town where I thought I'd forgotten my purse the night before. When I got to the hotel where I had been staying, I found out it was actually in the trunk of my car. FML

Today, my boyfriend proposed to me in a really romantic way. After we called our parents to tell them the news, he turned to me and said, "Hey, I hope you know this doesn't mean you can start getting lazy in the sack." FML

Today, my boss fired me because he said I was spending too much time surfing the Internet. When I reminded him that my work computer isn't even networked, he said, "Oh, sorry, you're the one who takes too many smoke breaks." When I told him that I don't even smoke, he said, "Just go . . ." FML

Today, my family and I watched the video my dad took of me walking across the stage at my high school graduation. Turns out he recorded the wrong kid. FML

Today, my boyfriend started to plan our wedding. He included a clown. FML

Today, I spent hours cleaning the kitchen that my slob roommates always neglect. I scrubbed the floor, emptied the fridge, and washed all the dishes. When I was done, I got myself a soda. When I opened the can, it exploded and sprayed everything I had just washed. FML

Today, I am nine months pregnant. I had a dream where I successfully pushed and gave birth to my son. Meanwhile, in the real world, I had successfully pushed and given birth to a large dump. FML

Today, my husband decided he will be a "stay-at-home" dad. We have two cats. No kids. FML

Today, I got mugged by someone wearing a bear suit. FML

Today, someone broke into my car to steal $1.50. FML

Today, I finally convinced my son to use the potty. Later, he saw a show on TV about a toilet monster. Now he's too scared to even step foot into the bathroom. Here's to another few months of diaper changes. FML

Today, I discovered that I'm allergic to adhesive bandages. I now have a bandage-shaped rash around a tiny cut on my leg. FML

Today, I was spelling T-R-E-A-T to my fiancé so that the dog couldn't understand what I was talking about. Turns out, neither could my fiancé. FML

Today, I spent hours fixing my favorite food for myself as a treat. While serving it, I made a mess that I wiped up with a napkin. I went to throw the napkin away on my way to the table. I looked down and was still holding the napkin. I had thrown the plate of food away instead. FML

Today, I was making out with my boyfriend. It was going well until our braces got caught. Out of pain, I tried to pull away, which made my eyes water. Then I proceeded to sneeze into his mouth. FML

Today, while running late to my sister's wedding and rushing to get ready, I accidentally grabbed my travel-size shaving cream in place of my body spray, and quickly drew a blue foaming line across my rental tux. FML

Today, I saw a video of myself I don't remember making last weekend. I was naked and pretending to be a duck. FML

Today, my little sister tripped when trying to walk up the stairs with a sandwich in one hand and my laptop in the other. She chose to save the sandwich. FML

Today, I found out I have dandruff when a random chick passed by and said out loud to her friends: "That dude's hair is having an early Christmas!" FML

Today, I was texting my boyfriend during a seven-hour car ride with my family. I thought it'd be fine to text dirty with him. Little did I know, my audio corrector was on, and it told me the right way to spell "penis" and "orgasm." We still had five hours left. FML

Today, after the graveyard shift at work, I took the bus home. I fell asleep on the way and woke up 25 miles away from my bus stop. I took another bus heading back and couldn't stay awake. I woke up where I started. FML

Today, I was working as a counselor at a special-needs camp when one parent asked another parent what my disorder was. FML

Today, I fell asleep in class. If that wasn't bad enough, I awoke gasping for air. I almost drowned in my arm fat. FML

Today, while house-sitting, I went to take my pizza out of the oven without realizing that the oven mitt had a hole in it. FML

Today, I swerved to avoid running over a dead cat in the road. Instead, I ran over its head. FML

Today, I learned two important facts: One, a grown man can, in fact, get beaten up by a teenage girl, and two, if someone is convinced you are someone else, there is no telling them otherwise. FML

Today, I realized my boyfriend only asks me to spend the night when he needs me to wake him up in the morning. FML

Today, my boyfriend gave me a pair of ankle weights for my birthday. FML

Today, while I was having sex with my boyfriend, he started pretending he was a dog. This included barking, licking my face, and scratching his ears. FML

Today, my family, including my two-year-old niece, went to the zoo. I held my niece at the lion exhibit so she could get a better view, and the lions roared. She got so scared that she peed. Her diaper wasn't very absorbent, but my shirt was. FML

Today, I was having sex with the guy I'm seeing. While I was having my orgasm, he looked at me and said, "SHHHH!" FML

Today, I learned my boyfriend has another girlfriend. His excuse was that he's bipolar and each of his personalities needs one. FML

Today, while me and my boyfriend were having sex, he moaned out his own name. FML

Today, I found out my boyfriend's mom still refers to his ex as the daughter she never had. FML

Today, my kitchen sink was clogged. I poured a bottle of drain cleaner down and came back two hours later. The clog is still there, but the glue on the pipe isn't, and now there's drain cleaner all over the floor, staining and dissolving everything in my kitchen. FML

Today, a couple of friends and I decided to go camping in a national park. When we got there, a ranger came up to us and said, "There have been many sightings of coyotes, but don't worry. If they charge at you, they'll bluff and flee at the last moment." We met a coyote; it didn't bluff. FML

Today, I learned that now that I have a tongue ring, it's a bad idea to test 9-volt batteries with my tongue. FML

Today, while I was driving, I saw my driving instructor from high school walking on the sidewalk. As I waved to him, I rear-ended the car in front of me. FML

Today, my wife decided to take my truck to a car wash as a surprise. As she was pulling out of the driveway, she ran over four sprinkler heads, flooding the yard, and took out our mailbox. FML

Today, I was eating pizza with my boyfriend and some friends. I was laughing and talking and went for another piece when my boyfriend grabbed my wrist and said that I had had enough. My friends all backed him up. FML

Today, I stopped at a yellow light. The guy behind me did not. He had no insurance. FML

Today, my girlfriend left me for my best friend—and told me in a text message with "lol" in it. FML

Today, my baby will only stop crying when I turn on the vacuum cleaner. I'm stuck with either a screaming baby or a roaring vacuum. FML

Today, I saw a guy crouched by my bike fiddling with something as I came out of a store. Thinking he was a thief, I slammed him across the head with my helmet and knocked him over. Then I realized that not only was he a kid barely in his teens, he was just tying his shoes. FML

Today, I realized that going back on birth control has made my acne go away and my boobs bigger. However, to my boyfriend's dismay, I've completely lost my sex drive. FML

Today, I realized my girlfriend snores loudest after amazing sex. I've tried earplugs, but sometimes I can't fall back to sleep. My choices are great sex and no sleep, or great sleep but no sex. FML

Today, I watched my boyfriend feed his cat and change his profile on both Myspace and Facebook before saying to me that he was "too busy to have sex." FML

Today, brushing my teeth took longer than sex with my boyfriend. FML

Today, I was jamming in a garage studio with people I had just met. After 20 minutes of playing what I thought was all right, the bass player walked over to my amplifier and unplugged my input cable. The rest of the band kept playing like nothing had happened. FML

Today, I took a picture of my boobs and sent it to my boyfriend, only to realize after I hit "send" that I had sent it to the taxi driver (my last phone call) who had just dropped me off at my house. He won't stop calling my phone now. FML

Today, the Jehovah's Witnesses were at my door. Normally I don't give them the time of day, but I was so lonely for company, I let them in. FML

Today, I was with my girlfriend. We thought we were alone in the house. Her little brother found us having sex on the couch, took a picture, and said, "You are now both my slaves." He ran upstairs and locked his bedroom door. FML

Today, I got a bill for the phone I got my son to use to call us from college. I found out he's been calling a phone sex hotline every day. He hasn't called us once. FML

Today, my girlfriend told me that I think too much during sex. Now the only thing I can think about is how much I'm thinking too much. FML

Today, I was having sex with my boyfriend. I was making a list of things to do tomorrow while faking an orgasm when I realized my boyfriend had finished about two minutes ago. He's pissed. FML

Today, I found out that I made inappropriate sexual comments to my boss while I was drunk on Saturday night. She won't tell me what I said. She just laughs when she sees me. FML

Today, when I was trying to break up with my boyfriend, I told him how I needed space and time to think. His response was, "Okay, we're out of condoms anyway." FML

Today, I had a phone interview with a college. The lady asked me to spell out my password so that she could access my test scores. The password was "dick." FML

Today, my sister's boyfriend came over to the house. I thought I would be nice and cook them both dinner. Mine took a little longer to cook, so they ate before me and went back to her bedroom. I ate alone to the sound of them having sex. FML

Today, I caught my dad spanking my mom with a spatula. The same spatula I use to cook my eggs every morning. FML

Today, I went to the grocery store, and I realized that all I bought was cat food and $30 worth of protein bars. Yes, I have become THAT single woman. FML

Today, my boyfriend told me he likes having sex during my period because it makes him feel like he stabbed a small animal to death. FML

Today, when I was complaining to my husband for spending way too much time in front of the TV, he pointed the remote control at me while miming turning down the volume. FML

Today, I sent a Facebook friend request to the guy who had the party I was at last night. I immediately realized, however, that my new profile picture is of me smiling and holding the trophy I stole from his house. FML

Today, I went on my first date in nearly a year. A few minutes into the meal, he called me "scrumptious" and proceeded to make animal noises for the rest of it. FML

Today, I stumbled upon my boyfriend's Facebook. His second account. On which I also stumbled upon his second girlfriend. FML

Today, my boyfriend and I were telling each other secrets. I told him I've shaved my upper lip. He said, "I know, it's prickly when we make out." FML

Today, I was on a blind date. We went to a fancy restaurant and she ordered the shrimp. I told her, "I'm allergic to shrimp, so you shouldn't order it in case I want to kiss you later." She looked at the waiter and said, "I'll have the shrimp." FML

Today, I was giving my parents a tour of my apartment when my bird started making noises. It was mimicking my moans from when I was having sex yesterday. It was very noticeably screaming in my voice. FML

Today, at lunch, I ordered a Coke. The waiter replied, "Diet Coke?" and I corrected him, saying, "No, regular Coke." He shook his head and said again, "Diet Coke." FML

PUERTO RICO

Today, after finally moving into a better neighborhood, my family and I were greeted by the elderly couple who live window to window to us. How? By hearing them have sex loudly and then pray for forgiveness even louder. Welcome to the neighborhood! FML

MEXICO

Today, I was blindsided at an intersection, sending my car flying and totaling it. The person who hit me said, "Sorry. I sneezed." FML

Today, my grandpa was wearing flip-flops and white socks. He entered my bathroom, and at the same moment I realized there was no toilet paper left. I felt too ashamed to interrupt his dump, so I waited for him to ask for a new roll. He never did, but he came out without socks. FML

Today, I noticed that my dog was feeling sad. I let him hop on my bed with me to make him feel better. It worked, right after he vomited all over my face and pillow. FML

Today, I was falling asleep on my desk, my head on my fist. My elbow slipped off the edge of the desk and I punched myself, leaving a fist mark on my cheek. At school, people think my parents hit me. My parents think I'm getting bullied at school. No one believes the actual story. FML

OCEANIA

AUSTRALIA

Today, my girlfriend randomly started to undo my belt buckle, unzip my fly, and take my pants off while we were watching TV. Right as I started to get really excited, she said, "Just kidding." FML

Today, I had my first appearance in court as an attorney. I called the prosecution "the prostitution." FML

Today, I was at a 21st birthday party. While the host blew out the candles, I whispered to the guy next to me, "That's not the only thing she will be blowing tonight." The guy next to me was her dad. FML

Today, I was playing one-on-one soccer with a girl I like. I accidentally kicked the ball right into her face. The ball rolled back toward me, and as I ran to see if she was okay, I kicked the ball . . . right into her face again. FML

Today, I took a bath with what I thought was my water-proof vibrator. It wasn't. Apparently, my boyfriend found me passed out in the tub from an electric shock with the vibrator floating next to me. FML

Today, I was at work at a sandwich store right next to a big hospital. There was a big line of people all getting their subs toasted. Without turning around, I said to the next person in line: "I bet you want yours extra toasted?" She was a burn victim from the hospital. FML

Today, it was my music recital. I sneezed really loud into my saxophone, which made the mouthpiece fly out of my mouth. When the neck strap was stretched as far as it would go, the saxophone came back toward me and hit me in the head. I knocked myself out in front of the audience. FML

Today, I got dumped because I was on my period. Apparently, he was pissed because I have one, "like, every single month." FML

Today, I was trying to convince my boyfriend that I am NOT a dumb blonde. After yelling at the top of my lungs, I proceeded to trip over a garbage can and hit my head on a wall. FML

Today, my husband came home from shopping with our four-year-old daughter and showed me a shirt she had picked out herself. The shirt read, "My mom's easy, I'm living proof." Apparently, she just liked the colors and her father agreed. FML

Today, after I spent a great evening with the guy I really like, he dropped me off outside my house. When he pulled into the driveway, his lights shone on my drunk mom taking out the garbage in her underwear. FML

Today, I went shopping with my boyfriend. I wore two bras under my tank top to make my chest look bigger. Upon leaving the store, one of the security guards noticed the extra straps and accused me of shoplifting. I had to spend the next 20 minutes explaining the situation to security. FML

Today, I bought an expensive dress because my boy-friend was taking me out for our one-year anniversary. When he saw me in the dress, he laughed and said, "Seriously, what are you wearing?" FML

Today, I found out that my girlfriend of five months is pregnant. Apparently, she stopped taking her pill two months ago because "we" wanted a baby. I don't recall ever having that discussion with her. FML

Today, I tested the new faucet in the shower using my head. Yep, it's strong enough. FML

Today, I have both a cold and my period. Tomorrow, I will have a cold, my period, and my wisdom teeth taken out. FML

Today, my sister decided to wake me up by pumping hand soap into my open mouth. FML

Today, my boyfriend wouldn't lick the whipped cream I had on my nipples because "that stuff is full of calories." FML

Today, I was expecting a call from my friend. The phone rang and I answered with "WANK!" as a joke. It wasn't my friend on the phone, it was my boss. FML

NEW ZEALAND

Today, I fell asleep and dreamed that I had won $500,000. In my dream, I used this money to buy a new MP3 player and then put the rest in a term deposit. Even in my dreams, I'm the most boring person I know. FML

Today, I decided to quit smoking. During my lunch break, I tried to ash a candy bar after I took a bite. FML

Today, while standing on the corner, I was squirted with a foreign liquid from a moving car. Turns out I got peed on. FML

Today, I flew my wife, myself, and three kids to pay a surprise visit to my parents, who were going to be alone for Christmas. When we arrived, we found out they had decided to go on vacation. We have nowhere to go. FML

Today, I found out that my friend uses pictures of me to motivate her to work out. They are accompanied by sayings such as "You don't want to turn out like this." FML

Today, I met up with a girl I've been talking to online for a year and a half. Turns out she edits her mustache out of all her photos. FML

Today, I was standing in the gas station, pulling out my wallet to pay for the $100 of gas I just filled my car with. I opened my wallet and found a note that said, "Borrowed money for food." FML

Today, I saw photos of my boyfriend at his 25th birthday party. The one he told me was canceled. FML

Today, I got back from vacation and realized I still had the motel key. The key ring has the address on it so you can send it back to them. I drove to the mailbox and threw the key in. I then discovered that the motel key won't start my car. FML

Today, my 11-year-old son and I were going through some old photos. He saw one of me when I was 22 on a beach wearing a bikini. He said, "Wow! Who's that?!" Quite proudly I said it was me. He looked at me and said, "What happened?!" FML

Today, at work, I noticed that my last pencil had been taken from my desk. I assumed it was the coworker who I've talked to at least 10 times regarding taking my stationery. I approached her and, feeling brave, yelled at her in front of the entire office. Turns out I was holding the pencil. FML

Today, I met up with a guy from a local dating site for coffee. He walked up, looked me over, and said, "Ummm, no," then walked off. FML

Today, I was hanging out with some disabled people at the center where I work. We had the music blasting and were laughing and dancing around. My boss took me aside and said that it wasn't really appropriate for me to mock the clients by imitating their dancing. That's just how I dance. FML

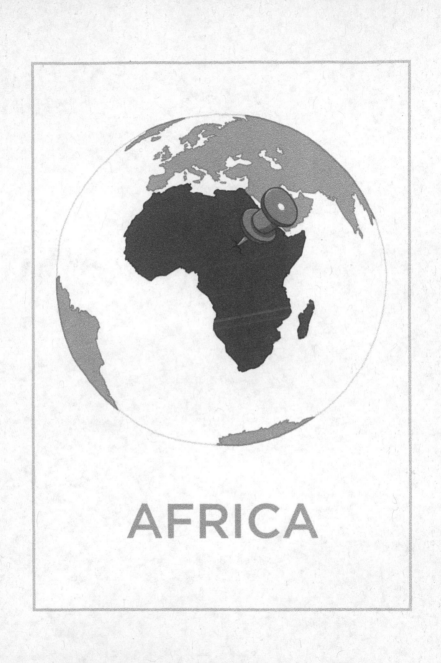

AFRICA

EGYPT

Today, I decided to have sex for the first time with my boyfriend. It was his first time, too. While in bed, he blankly stopped and stood up and got out a piece of paper from his pocket. Turns out, he had written instructions on what to do while in bed, and forgot what he had to do next. FML

SOUTH AFRICA

Today, a customer came into the music shop where I work to look at guitars. After calling the customer "Dude" and "Man" numerous times, I watched them stalk off suddenly. When I asked if everything was okay, they responded with, "I'm female, you asshole!" FML

Today, at my bachelorette party, I got so wasted, I ended up giving my stripper a lap dance because he wasn't "doing it properly." There are photos. FML

Today, while I was in the shower, my roommates thought it would be really funny if they threw my cat in with me. The doctor who gave me the stitches also thought so. FML

Today, I was texting a friend. She mentioned it was her dad's birthday. I typed, "Tell him Happy Birthday for me!" and as I pressed send I remembered her dad was dead. FML

Today, while driving on a totally deserted, long, straight road in the middle of nowhere, I sneezed and drove right into a pole on the side of the road. It was the only pole for 30 miles. FML

F MY LIFE
WORLD TOUR EXCLUSIVES

These never-before-seen entries were submitted on our French site, VieDeMerde.fr. Here's your chance to be among the first to laugh at someone else's expense!

Today, while working as a policeman, I met an awesome woman. We had a great date, up until I opened the car door for her and, out of habit, put my hand on her head as she got in. FML

Today, I picked up the 10 cotton shirts that I'd had made using a shirt I gave to a tailor as a template. The guy made me 10 identical shirts, right down to the cigarette hole in each left sleeve. FML

Today, my dog was scratching his neck. Trying to be nice, I scratched it for him. Two seconds later, he scratched his paw, and I scratched it in turn. He then licked his balls and looked at me again. I wonder if he did it deliberately. FML

Today, the guy I've been in love with for two years finally spoke to me, only to tell me to "shut the fuck up." FML

Today, my turtle, who had a little portion of the garden all to herself, died. My five-year-old nephew wanted to "be like Mario" by jumping on her. FML

Today, I was video chatting with my boyfriend. I started to put on a saucy mini-show when he suddenly said, "My mother thinks you have nice boobs." FML

Today, an astrology website informed me that, according to my name and birth date, my lucky day will be February 30. This explains a lot. FML

Today, I put my ironing board away in the bathroom. After closing the door, I heard a loud noise. The board had opened up while falling over, taking up the width of the room. Now I can't open the door. FML

Today, it's been two days since my upstairs neighbor's toilet started flooding. I have to go to the bathroom with an umbrella. FML

Today, I was in a really bad mood. When I got home, I gave what I thought was my son's fuzzy toy a huge kick. Our poodle can really fly. FML

Today, as revenge for a prank, a friend drew on my bathroom mirror with toothpaste. Dried toothpaste is difficult to clean, so I used steel wool. Now I have a huge dick and balls engraved into my mirror. FML

Today, I learned a lot about my upstairs neighbor's life. That he's a fan of hard-core techno is one thing. That his bed makes a racket when he has sex is another. But when he combines the two, it's too much to take. FML

Today, we were playing a guessing game in my dorm room involving finding out what is written on bits of paper stuck to our heads. The RA stopped by to tell us we were making too much noise. I answered the door, unaware that on my forehead was a note that said, "Russian whore." FML

Today, during the night, my girlfriend murmured into my ear: "Are you asleep?" To test her reaction, I didn't reply. She then let out a loud and rancid fart, shook the sheets while giggling, and went back to sleep. FML

Today, while trying to jump over a subway turnstile, I hit my leg on it, put my hands forward to avoid splitting my nose on the floor, and got stuck upside down between the turnstile and the door. FML

Today, my piece of toast fell butter-side up for a change. Too bad my dog got to it before I could. FML

Today, while moving my couch to clean, I found the answers to three conundrums: Where did my cat get his food last week? Where did the fish I was supposed to eat during the week go? Where was that awful smell coming from? FML

Today, I ran into my ob-gyn and her husband at a party. A bit embarrassed, I shook their hands and introduced myself as a patient. She turned to her husband and said, "Oh, I told you about her! She has a perfect vagina, such a magnificent opening!" I was no longer embarrassed; I was mortified. FML

Today, I told my mother that I'm gay. She just said, "Very well," in her stuck-up upper-class way, before passing out. FML

Today, unable to find the potato masher, my husband put all the boiled potatoes in a plastic bag and drove over them with the front wheel of the car. FML

Today, I found out that my colleagues replaced my email auto-responder message with "This is Christopher. I'll be away for two weeks. When I get back from Brazil, due to the surgery, please address me by my new name: Crystal." FML

Today, during a skiing lesson, I felt the urge to pee. The instructor pointed to some bushes. When I got behind them, I dropped my pants and underwear, only to start sliding down the hill. Unable to stop, I slid out from behind the bushes and landed on my bare behind, next to the rest of the class, who was waiting for me on the slope. FML

Today, I met up with a lady who found my lost dog in the street. I arrived feeling excited, but she turned up empty-handed. She said, "Yes, he'd started to smell bad, so I buried him." I didn't know he was dead. FML

Today, as I was entering my date's number into my phone, I was unable to remember his name. Embarrassed, I tried to be sneaky and asked, "Can you spell your name, please?" His name is Bob. FML

Today, it's been two months since I got a kitten. He loves to hide and then surprise me by jumping out of his hiding place. It was quite a surprise when he launched himself out of my backpack during class. FML

Today, I bought a curtain rod. When I was in the subway, I held it vertically, and everyone seemed to think it was a subway pole. Imagine the faces of the six people hanging on to my curtain rod when the subway arrived at my stop. FML

Today, at a nightclub, I noticed a cute guy was staring at me. Happy to be hit on, I danced like crazy on the dance floor, all the while staring seductively back. I ended up going over to talk to him. It was a photograph on a wall. I was hit on by a poster. FML

Today, I had a drunken night in a loft with lots of people. My wife pulled me into the bathroom and we had wild sex. Later in the evening, she spotted me and jumped into my arms, saying, "Oh, honey, you finally made it!" I was cheated on by myself. FML

Today, I returned home to my parents' house, drunk. Feeling hungry, I grabbed a slice of bread and some butter and took a few bites. Five hours later, my mother woke me up and dragged me to the kitchen. In the middle of the table was a buttered, half-eaten sponge. FML

Today, one of my husband's old college buddies came to dinner. Talking about our college days, he laughingly remembered that my husband had a fake friend called Marc Deveau he'd say he was with when cheating on his girlfriend. My husband still sees Marc Deveau. FML

Today, I was visiting my grandmother with my new girlfriend. We were drinking coffee when my Granny leaned to one side and let out a huge fart. Proud of herself, she added, "That one didn't pay his rent on time!" Coffee came out of my girlfriend's nose. FML

Today, I was sleepwalking. During the night, I apparently grabbed my mother's hair and demanded to know "where the lost penguin's country is." FML

Today, while out jogging, I came across a Yorkshire terrier who wouldn't stop barking. Having been bitten before, I used my tried and tested dog-scaring technique: scream as loud as possible while putting my arms in the air like an ogre. The dog dropped dead. Its elderly owner was devastated. FML

Today, my girlfriend looked through the contents of my refrigerator and started with her usual "You're a pig, you never clean up" routine. She said, "Look at this egg, it makes me want to throw up, it's black, covered in fur, AND THERE'S EVEN HAIR ON IT!" I took a look: It was a kiwi. FML

Today, during my first day as a medical intern in a new ward, I was doing a rectal exam when my chief resident, as a prank, burst in screaming, "Who are you?! You're not even a doctor, you pervert!" FML

Today, during my fifth attempt to pass my driving test, my inspector noticed the four previous marks on the form and said, "Did you think it was a customer loyalty card or something?" FML

Today, I farted during a job interview. After a short, uncomfortable pause, I said, "It wasn't me." FML

Today, I was alone watching the only TV we have at home, located in my parents' bedroom. I'm not allowed to watch it during the afternoon, so when they came home early, I hid under their bed to avoid trouble. I never should've done that. Never. FML

Today, I gave birth to my daughter in the hospital hallway. The nurse who took me up to my room afterward tried to comfort me by saying, "There's been worse; two years ago a lady gave birth in the parking lot." That was me, too. FML

Today, I was in the break room with my colleagues and our awful boss. As usual, he was talking trash and was totally convinced his jokes were funny. The window was open, and it was chilly. As he walked by it, I mangled my words and said, "Cedric, could you please shut your mouth?" FML

Today, desperate after a very painful breakup, I poured my heart and soul out to my old teddy bear. When I finished, I asked what he would do in my situation. Right on cue, a gust of wind came through the window and sent him falling off the windowsill and crashing headfirst onto the floor. FML

Today, while camping, upon returning from the bathroom, I found my boyfriend at the other end of the tent, naked, on all fours, looking for something. Feeling frisky, I slipped my hand between his legs and said to him, "Who do these belong to?" I was in the wrong tent. FML

Today, my wife's friend asked her what she uses for contraception. I clearly heard my wife answer, "World of Warcraft." FML

Today, I felt for the first time the side effects of the medicine I'm taking, which causes me to become very emotional. I started crying in front of my girlfriend because she didn't want to put grated cheese on her pasta. FML

Today, I went bungee jumping for the first time. I was pretty nervous about it. After a few instructions, I was ready to go. I crept out to the launchpad, dangled my toes into the air, and bent my knees, ready to jump, before I heard, "WAIT! She's not attached!" I almost had a stroke. FML

Today, my aunt walked in on her dog eating the parrot that she'd been looking after. To punish him, she put what was left of the parrot into the freezer and now and then hits the dog with the frozen bird, shouting, "Look at what you did!" FML

Today, as a way of grading my work, my history teacher simply wrote "LOL" at the top of the paper. FML

Today, I went on a first date with a colleague. I endured a three-hour walk around Paris, a two-hour dinner, a one-and-a-half-hour movie, 45 minutes for a "nightcap," 30 minutes of passionate kissing, 20 minutes of fore-play, and 20 seconds of penetration. FML

Today, I had to learn a scene from a play, and the only quiet place to do so was in the bathroom. I felt bad for my colleague, who overheard me saying, "This time you've gone too far; you have to go." *Splash* FML

Today, as usual, my husband sent me to fill up his water bottle for the night. Being a good wife, I went to the bathroom to do so. I crossed paths with my six-year-old daughter, who said to me wearily, "Boys are all the same: lazy." She was filling her brother's bottle. FML

Today, it's been three days since I ran into my boyfriend's scantily clad sister in his apartment. Today, I realized that he doesn't have a sister. FML

Today, our son asked for a laptop. We agreed that if he could come up with a good reason to get one, we'd think about it. He said he wants one so he can "keep watching movies while taking a shit." He's already convinced his father. FML

Today, I took a shower with my girlfriend. It started to get kinky, and she said to me in an erotic tone: "Punish me." The only thing I could think of doing was to rub soap in her eyes. FML

Today, I heard my parents arguing in the next room. It's been a while since they decided to get a divorce, and now they're arguing about who doesn't have to get custody of me. FML

Today, I heard my sister masturbating with my electric toothbrush. She put it back on its stand as if nothing was wrong. FML

Today, I ran into an old friend. I asked her how she was doing, and said, "And your mom?" I then remembered that she'd died a few years ago, so trying to save face, I added without thinking, ". . . still in the same graveyard?" FML

Today, a guy was sitting opposite me on the subway. I checked him out, noticed he was reading a book on philosophy, and found him completely to my liking. Just as I was about to talk to him, he looked up from his book and said coldly, "Don't even try." FML

Today, I was trying to do homework when my neighbor started playing loud heavy metal music. Annoyed, I knocked on his door to demand he stop. It turns out some stereotypes are true: six feet tall, 200 pounds, a beard, and long hair. I ended up asking if I could borrow some sugar. FML

Today, my six-year-old son was watching children's TV. On a commercial, a cartoon character said, "Eat your fruit and vegetables; they'll help you grow, and they're delicious, too!" To which my son shot back, "You think I'm stupid?!" FML

Today, my five-year-old son was talking to our elderly neighbor in the elevator. I always lectured my son on the importance of being polite, so I was pleased when he said, "Good-bye, sir! See you next time!" Then he added in the same tone, "Well, if you're still alive!" FML

Today, I was struggling to cycle up a steep hill. A guy heading past me on a scooter said I'd lost something. I stopped and looked back. Seeing nothing, I asked him what I'd lost. He replied, "Your momentum!" FML

Today, I'm faced with a dilemma: Either I keep quiet about having seen a picture of my math teacher on a gay dating site, or I explain to the class what I was doing on a gay dating site. FML

Today, while in a changing room at the pool, I saw a hole in the wall to the other room. As anyone would have, I looked through the hole. What did I see? An eye. FML

Today, my girlfriend and I were playing around and throwing stuffed animals at each other. Short on ammo, I saw a teddy bear sticking out from the foot of the bed. I grabbed it and threw it at her. It was her cat. FML

Today, I was invited to eat over at my girlfriend's parents' house. When her father told me how proud he was that his daughter was still a virgin, I couldn't help but audibly snicker. FML

Today, I woke up in an unusually good mood, got up, did my morning exercises, took a shower, sang happily, got dressed, opened my bedroom window, and felt a wad of bird shit slam straight into my face. FML

Today, I received a letter from my boyfriend. Overjoyed, I ran up the stairs to my bedroom, telling myself, "Stop grinning. You look stupid, and it's probably just a breakup letter!" It was. FML

Today, on the subway, a woman got off without her suitcase. I grabbed the case, chased her onto the platform,
and shouted, "You forgot your suitcase!" while the doors
closed behind me. It, in fact, wasn't her suitcase, and its
actual owner was still on the train. FML

**Today, I noticed my boyfriend's online status
said, "Over at Elisa's." I looked at hers, only
to see, "In bed." FML**

Today, my friend showed me a picture of the house he
just finished building. He said, "And in the back is the
garden and swimming pool." I turned the photo over,
looking for them. FML

**Today, my very shy girlfriend finally indulged two of my
fantasies. She gave me a striptease and blindfolded me.
Both at the same time. FML**

Today, I awoke with a start. Realizing I'd forgotten to feed my cat, I jumped out of bed and rushed down the stairs. After a few steps, I tripped and fell down on the tile floor. Pained and stunned, I remembered I don't have a cat. FML

Today, while driving home, I came across a sheep lying in the middle of the road. When I got out and checked to see if it was hurt, it bit me and ran away. FML

Today, I went online to search for help with a personal problem. As I wrote in my search query, a friend IM'd me, asking, "Hey, how are you?" My unintentional response: "Serious vaginal discharge." FML

Today, my five-year-old daughter came home from school. It was cold and she was very tired. I said, "Take off your socks and blow your nose." She took off her socks and blew her nose into them. FML

Today, I was playing an intense game on my computer. Having beaten my score, I thrust my arms in the air victoriously. I found out my boss had been standing behind me the whole time when one of my fists slammed into his nose. FML

Today, I woke up to the sight of my boyfriend's magnificent ass. I couldn't resist giving it a light slap. He then slapped me, causing my head to slam back against the wall. I lay there stunned for 20 minutes while he kept pleading, "I thought it was a wasp!" FML

Today, I dressed up as Santa Claus for our company's family holiday party. When my daughter's turn arrived, she sat on my lap, put her lips to my ear, and whispered softly: "I want a new dad." FML

Today, I saw a pretty girl about to light up a cigarette. I hurried over and said, "They say women who smoke are anything but attractive." She replied, "They also say lesbians shouldn't care what men think of them." FML

Today, while I was singing my son to sleep, he took the pacifier from his mouth and put it in mine. FML

Today, I knew that I must have a very interesting life ahead of me, because I dreamed that my Prince Charming was a potato peeler. FML

Today, my 15-year-old son told me he wants to get another dentist. His reasoning is that "it's too hard to see her huge breasts at every checkup and not be able to touch them." FML

Today, I was eating a kebab in the subway. A kid in front of me was loudly and messily eating a chocolate crêpe. His mother looked at him, then at me, and asked, "Are you two having an eating contest?" FML

Today, I found out my boss didn't sleep with my wife. He's sleeping with my daughter. FML

Today, my five-year-old daughter told me she was going to throw up. I told her to rush to the bathroom. I followed her a few minutes later, only to find her sitting on the toilet and vomiting onto the floor. FML

Today, I went to the movies. A cute guy who was sitting two seats away approached me and whispered, "Excuse me, I don't usually do this, but could I ask you . . ." (At which point I was already smiling.) ". . . could you please put your shoes back on?" FML

Today, I was making love with my girlfriend. I was really into it, but then I noticed she was quiet and staring blankly at the ceiling. I asked her if she was bored. She replied, "Oh, sorry!" and went back to making the usual moans. FML

Today, I was feeling extremely tired, so I asked my husband to take our son to school. At the end of the day, I went to pick my son up. He was still dressed in his pajamas. FML

Today, it was sunny outside, so I opened my apartment window. As soon as I did, a pigeon flew through and into my living room. Panicked, it flew around wildly, knocking over everything in its path. I tried to get it to fly out by opening all the other windows. Another pigeon flew in. FML

Today, I tricked my 12-year-old son into thinking I'd accidentally deleted his World of Warcraft account, just so I could see his reaction. He completely lost his shit and started hitting me. FML

Today, I tried hinting to my husband that we needed a new washing machine. I mentioned that we got our current one way back on our wedding day. He replied, "Yeah, it's time for a few trade-ins." FML

Today, I watched *The Bridges of Madison County* with my boyfriend, and all through the film, I tried to hold back my tears. In the end, I sniffled one last time. I was relieved that he didn't notice. Then he turned, looked me in the eyes with tears in his own, and said accusingly, "Don't you have a heart?!" FML

Today, a friend told me over instant messaging that his father had died. Trying to express some solidarity, I went to send him a tearful smiley. I accidentally sent him the dancing pig animation instead. FML

Today, my boyfriend sent me a text message saying, "I'm thinking of you." Flattered and feeling in the mood, I asked, "What are you doing?" He replied, "Taking a shit." FML

Today, I woke up hungover and blond. Yesterday, I was sober and brunette. FML

Today, I was sitting at my desk and talking to a client. I was idly swinging my feet and accidentally hit the lever on the chair. Throughout the conversation, I gradually disappeared from her field of vision. She's probably still laughing at me. FML

Today, I was walking my dog. I called, and he came over, whimpering and sheepish. He had a water bottle between his hind legs. His penis was stuck in it. FML

Today, I had an upset stomach. I lay down in bed, with a bucket nearby just in case. Later on, the urge to vomit overcame me, and I puked into the bucket. I realized too late that my cat had chosen to sleep in it. He jumped out and splattered vomit all over my apartment. FML

Today, I visited a friend in the hospital who was recovering after losing a finger in an accident. In an effort to cheer him up, I brought him cookies. Only after handing them to him did I realize they were Vienna Fingers. FML

Today, my kids decided to make a snowman in the backyard. After about 20 minutes, they came inside and asked for a carrot and a pair of oranges. They didn't put them on the part of the body I'd expected. FML

Today, while I was peacefully sleeping, I felt a hand suddenly slap my forehead. Then fingers began to press against my mouth, then nose, then eyes. I finally woke up to my girlfriend laughing hysterically. She'd confused my face with her clock radio. FML

Today, I was at a party with some friends when I decided to grab my girlfriend and throw her into the pool. It was empty. FML

Today, I was taking my driving test. Everything went well until the very last corner, where I saw my parents standing and holding up a banner that read, "You can do it, sweetie!" FML

Today, I was scheduled to give a presentation to my class. As I arrived, my teacher said to me, "You're bleeding from the 120th pimple on your left cheek." FML

Today, a complete stranger ran up to me, slapped me across the face, and yelled, "That's for stealing my pencil at school!" I'm 23 years old. FML

Today, I discovered that while I was sleeping, my lover had written a message to my husband on my ass. FML

Today, I realized that my husband says the same things to me during sex as he does to our baby daughter when he feeds her: "It's good, isn't it?" "You like that, don't you?" "Oh, you greedy girl!" FML

Today, my boyfriend was rushed to the ER because of kidney pains. The nurse made a point of massaging his balls for what seemed like an eternity before saying, "Better get a doctor down here; I don't know what I'm doing." FML

Today, I was at my girlfriend's house with her parents. During a lull in the conversation, I noticed everyone was staring at me. Covering myself while I thought of something to say, I grabbed an apple from the fruit bowl and took a bite. It was plastic. FML

Today, I got stuck in a hospital elevator from 10:30 to 11:45. I'm now the proud father of a daughter named Maria. She was born at 10:55. FML

Today, I had a swollen knee and was slowly limping to the bathroom. All of a sudden, my mom ran past me, beating me there. As she closed the door, she said, "AT LEAST I CAN RUN!" FML

Today, I broke my little toe. It got stuck in my underwear as I struggled to get a leg through. FML

Today, the farmer next door invited me over and offered to give me a rabbit. I sent my kids to choose one from the hutch, and they pointed out the one they found the cutest. She then opened the hutch, grabbed the rabbit by the ears, and cut its throat, all while giving me cooking tips. FML

Today, one of the lenses of my glasses cracked after being struck by a gummy bear that someone dropped from the top of the Eiffel Tower. FML

Today, my daughter and I walked into the waiting room at the doctor's office. Two guys were already there, and my daughter kept staring at them. Five minutes later, she loudly asked, "Mommy, which one's stinking so bad?" FML

Today, my family and I were watching a video they made of my birth. When my mom saw me for the first time, she audibly exclaimed, "He's really ugly!" FML

Today, and for the tenth time this week, a group of cats kept meowing just below my bedroom window. Pissed off, I got up, grabbed my glass of water, and threw the contents out the window. Tomorrow, I'll try again; this time with the window open. FML

Today, I was preparing dinner for my in-laws for the first time. Nervous, I accidentally spilled the pasta into the sink. With nothing else to prepare, I quickly scooped it all back out. Nobody would have been the wiser, if the kitchen sponge hadn't shown up in the middle of the meal. FML

Today, my mom found out that I smoke. How? When they mentioned on the news that the price of cigarettes is going up, I grumbled, "Christ, not again." FML

Today, I finally convinced my husband to sort his laundry into appropriate piles, so the colors wouldn't mix. When he finished, he showed me the two piles he'd made. One marked "Really dirty," and another marked "Not too dirty," which he could "wear one more time." FML

Today, my five-year-old cousin was bored and wanted to play tag. I was totally uninterested, so I told her to come up with her own version of the game, just to surprise me. Five minutes later, I was bleeding from the leg. She tagged me with a fork. FML

Today, I decided to shave my balls. When I was finished, I vacuumed up the mess on the carpet, and then the fragments of hair still on my balls. Very bad idea. FML

ACKNOWLEDGMENTS

In this book, there are many gems. But in the same way nuggets of gold are found, you can't just bend down to pick them up. You have to dig really deep. So we are really grateful for the wonderful work that Julien Azarian and Alan Holding achieve, helping us to sift through an enormous volume of the submissions every day, and finding the ones that shine the brightest.

ABOUT THE AUTHORS

Maxime Valette was born on April 30, 1988, in Reims, France. He can't remember a time when he didn't have a computer within arm's reach. He started developing programs at age nine, building websites at eleven, created an association at fifteen, one of whose activities became a viable business when he was sixteen, which he sold at eighteen to create the original FML website, VieDeMerde .fr (did everyone catch all of that?). Besides computers, his hobbies include music (playing the cello for the past ten years) and wine (he lives in the region where Champagne is made).

Guillaume Passaglia was born January 28, 1982, somewhere on the Côte d'Azur. He likes polar bears and vodka martinis (shaken, not stirred). He's also a developer, photographer, and sporting legend. He was a longtime online gamer but now enjoys other games such as directing several international-level companies. He never takes a break. He's also in charge of the housework around the apartment that the FML team uses for meetings. He likes things to be perfect. His ultimate dream is to one day beat Didier Guedj at tennis.

Didier Guedj was born in Paris a long time ago. After studying international business and starting a career in marketing, he went on to compose advertising jingles before becoming a creative director, designing campaigns for several ad agencies, and eventually establishing his own agency. From Heineken to Canon, various French perfumes and bestselling books, he has worked on more than 100 ad campaigns. He's the devil.

ABOUT THE ILLUSTRATOR

Marie Levesque (Missbean) was born on September 6 in Paris. After three years studying architecture, she now works full-time on illustrations in a house in the countryside, which is full of mosquito-hunting spiders. Marie likes beer and chocolate, and loves taking pictures of insects up close and watching movies while sleeping—this is why she never remembers the endings.